Cursive Handwriting Workbook For Teens

This book belongs to:

Gianna Carroll

Today is going to be a good day.

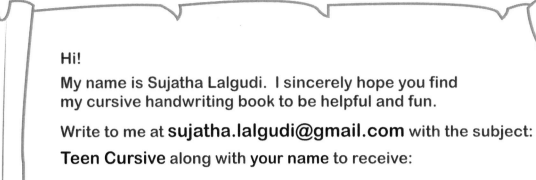

Hi!

My name is Sujatha Lalgudi. I sincerely hope you find my cursive handwriting book to be helpful and fun.

Write to me at **sujatha.lalgudi@gmail.com** with the subject:

Teen Cursive along with **your name** to receive:

- Additional practice worksheets.
- A name tracing worksheet to inspire you to create your
- own signature.
- An Award Certificate in Color to reward yourself!

Thank you
Sujatha Lalgudi

Part 1:
Learning Letters

Trace the letters and practice writing them
in the remaining space!

Practice tracing the letters in a smaller size at the end.
You can try writing on your own on the blank sheets at
the end!

Are you ready?
Let's go!

a a a a a a a

a a a a a a a

a a a a a a a a a a a a a a a a a a a

a a a a a a a a a a a a a a a a a a a a a a

a a a a a a a a a a a a a a a a a a a a a a a a

a a a a a a

a a a a a a

a a a a a a a a a a a a a a a a a a

a a a a a a a a a a a a a a a a a a a a

a a a a a a a a a a a a a a a a a a a a a a a

b   b   b   b   b   b
b   b   b   b   b   b

b b b b b b b b b b b
b b b b b b b b b b b

B   B   B   B   B
B   B   B   B   B

B B B B B B

B

c c c c c c

c c c c c c

c

c

C C C C C

C C C C C

C

C

d   d   d   d   d   d

d   d   d   d   d   d

d

d

D   D   D   D   D

D   D   D   D   D

D

D

e   e   e   e   e   e

e   e   e   e   e   e

e

e

E   E   E   E   E

E   E   E   E   E

E

E

f f f f f f

F F F F F

g g g g g g g

g g g g g g g

g

g

G G G G G G

G G G G G G

G

G

h h h h h h h

h h h h h h h

h

h

H H H H H H H

H H H H H H H

H

H

i

1 2 3 4

i i i i i i

i i i i i i

i

i

l

3 2 1 4

l l l l l

l l l l l

l

l

j

j j j j j j

j j j j j j

j

j

J

J J J J J

J J J J J

J

J

k k k k k k

k k k k k k

k

k

K K K K K K

K K K K K K

K

K

l l l l l l l
l l l l l l

L L L L L
L L L L L

m m m m
m m m m

m

m

m m m m
m m m m

m

m

n   *m*   *m*   *m*   *m*

m   *m*   *m*   *m*   *m*

m

m

n   *n*   *n*   *n*   *n*

n   *n*   *n*   *n*   *n*

n

n

p p p p p p p

p p p p p p p

p

p

p p p p p p p

p p p p p p p

P

P

q q q q q q q
q q q q q q

q
q

Q Q Q Q Q
Q Q Q Q Q

Q

Q

r n n n n n

n n n n n n

n

n

R R R R R

R R R R R

R

R

s

𝒮

t   t   t   t   t   t   t

t   t   t   t   t   t   t

t

t

T   T   T   T   T   T

T   T   T   T   T

T

T

u u u u u u u

u u u u u u u

u

u

U U U U U

U U U U U

U

U

n n n n n n

n n n n n n

n

n

v v v v v v

v v v v v v

v

v

w   nv   nv   nv

nv   nv   nv   nv

nv

nv

W   W   W   W

W   W   W   W

W

W

a b c d e f g h i j k l m n o p q r s t u v w x y z

x x x x x

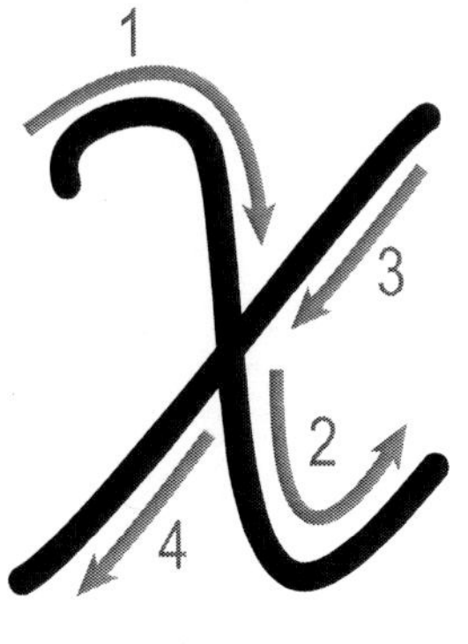

X X X X X

A B C D E F G H I J K L M N O P Q R S T U V W X Y Z

y y y y y

y y y y y

y

y

Y Y Y Y Y

Y Y Y Y Y

Y

Y

abcdefghijklmnopqrstuvwxyz

abcdefghijklmmop

qrstuvwwxyz

abcdefghijklmmop

qrstuvwwxyz

abcdefghijklmmop

qrstuvwwxyz

abcdefghijklmmop

qrstuvwwxyz

ABCDEFGHIJKLMNOPQRSTUVWXYZ

a b c d e f g h i j k l m n o p q r s t u v w x y z

A B C D E F G H I J K L M
N O P Q R S T U V W X Y Z
A B C D E F G H I J K L M
N O P Q R S T U V W X Y Z
A B C D E F G H I J K L M
N O P Q R S T U V W X Y Z
A B C D E F G H I J K L M
N O P Q R S T U V W X Y Z

A B C D E F G H I J K L M N O P Q R S T U V W X Y Z

Aa Bb Cc Dd Ee Ff Gg Hh Ii

Jj Kk Ll Mm Nn Oo Pp Qq Rr

Ss Tt Uu Vv Ww Xx Yy Zz

Aa Bb Cc Dd Ee Ff Gg Hh Ii

Jj Kk Ll Mm Nn Oo Pp Qq Rr

Ss Tt Uu Vv Ww Xx Yy Zz

Aa Bb Cc Dd Ee Ff Gg Hh Ii

Jj Kk Ll Mm Nn Oo Pp Qq Rr

Ss Tt Uu Vv Ww Xx Yy Zz

ABCDEFGHIJKLMNOPQRSTUVWXYZ

Part 2: Words

Two, three, four letter words & capitalization

We will now practice writing words using a smaller letter size.

Trace the words and practice writing them in the remaining space!

You are AMAZING!

an an an an an an

be be be be be be

do do do do do do

go go go go go go

hi hi hi hi hi hi

if if if if if if

lo lo lo lo lo lo

my my my my my

no no no no no no

on on on on on on

pi pi pi pi pi pi

so so so so so so

to to to to to to

us us us us us us

we we we we we we

Write your own words here:

a i n air air air air

bag bag bag bag bag

can can can can can

did did did did did

eel eel eel eel eel

far far far far far

got got got got got

has has has has has

key key key key key

lid lid lid lid lid

mat mat mat mat mat

met met met met met

oil oil oil oil oil

pro pro pro pro pro

rug rug rug rug rug

say say say say say

nam nan nan nan nan

web web web web web

yet yet yet yet yet

gap gap gap gap gap

Write your own words here:

able able able able able

bold bold bold bold bold

Write your own words here:

crew crew crew crew crew

dawn dawn dawn dawn

even even even even even

farm farm farm farm farm

good good good good good

hand hand hand hand hand

idle   idle   idle   idle   idle

joke   joke   joke   joke   joke

Write your own words here:

kind   kind   kind   kind   kind

list   list   list   list   list

mine   mine   mine   mine   mine

nest   nest   nest   nest   nest

oven   oven   oven   oven   oven

part   part   part   part   part

quit quit quit quit quit

roar roar roar roar roar

Write your own words here:

sand sand sand sand sand

time time time time time

used used used used used

vent vent vent vent vent

work work work work work

x-ray x-ray x-ray x-ray

year year year year year

zoom zoom zoom zoom

Write your own words here:

At At At At At

Bus Bus Bus Bus Bus

Can Can Can Can Can

Dog Dog Dog Dog Dog

Ear Ear Ear Ear Ear

Far Far Far Far Far

Gum Gum Gum Gum

Had Had Had Had

If If If If If

Jog Jog Jog Jog Jog

Kim Kim Kim Kim Kim

Lit Lit Lit Lit Lit

Met Met Met Met

Not Not Not Not Not

Odd Odd Odd Odd Odd

Pay Pay Pay Pay Pay

Quiz Quiz Quiz Quiz

Rug Rug Rug Rug Rug

Sun Sun Sun Sun Sun

Top Top Top Top Top

Use Use Use Use Use

Vest Vest Vest Vest Vest

Win Win Win Win Win

Xenon Xenon Xenon Xenon

Yak Yak Yak Yak Yak

Zoom Zoom Zoom Zoom

Write your own words here:

Part 3:
Number Words & Calendar Words

We will now practice writing numbers and number words.

Trace the dotted numbers and number words, then write them in the remaining space.
Use your best handwriting!

Fantastic!

1 2 3 4 5 6 7 8 9 10

1 2 3 4 5 6 7 8 9 10

1 2 3 4 5 6 7 8 9 10

1 2 3 4 5 6 7 8 9 10

1 2 3 4 5 6 7 8 9 10

1 2 3 4 5 6 7 8 9 10

11 12 13 14 15 16 17 18 19 20

21 22 23 24 25 26 27 28 29 30

31 32 33 34 35 36 37 38 39 40

41 42 43 44 45 46 47 48 49 50

51 52 53 54 55 56 57 58 59 60

61 62 63 64 65 66 67 68 69 70

71 72 73 74 75 76 77 78 79 80

81 82 83 84 85 86 87 88 89 90

91 92 93 94 95 96 97 98 99 100

Numbers

1 2 3 4 5 6 7 8 9 10 11 12 13 14 15 16

17 18 19 20 21 22 23 24 25 26 27 28

29 30 31 32 33 34 35 36 37 38 39 40

41 42 43 44 45 46 47 48 49 50 51 52

53 54 55 56 57 58 59 60 61 62 63 64

65 66 67 68 69 70 71 72 73 74 75 76

77 78 79 80 81 82 83 84 85 86 87 88

89 90 91 92 93 94 95 96 97 98 99 100

100 200 300 400 500 600 700 800

900 1000

Numbers

One One One One One One

Two Two Two Two Two Two

Three Three Three Three Three

Four Four Four Four Four

Five Five Five Five Five

Six Six Six Six Six Six

Seven Seven Seven Seven

Eight Eight Eight Eight Eight

Nine Nine Nine Nine Nine

Ten Ten Ten Ten Ten Ten

Eleven   Eleven   Eleven

Twelve   Twelve   Twelve

Thirteen   Thirteen   Thirteen

Fourteen   Fourteen   Fourteen

Fifteen   Fifteen   Fifteen

Sixteen   Sixteen   Sixteen

Seventeen   Seventeen

Eighteen   Eighteen   Eighteen

Nineteen   Nineteen   Nineteen

Twenty   Twenty   Twenty

Twenty-one   Twenty-one   Twenty-one

Twenty-two   Twenty-two   Twenty-two

Twenty-three   Twenty-three

Twenty-four   Twenty-four   Twenty-four

Twenty-five   Twenty-five   Twenty-five

1 — One   11 — Eleven

2 — Two   12 — Twelve

3 — Three   13 — Thirteen

4 — Four   14 — Fourteen

5 — Five   15 — Fifteen

6 — Six   16 — Sixteen

7 — Seven   17 — Seventeen

8 — Eight   18 — Eighteen

9 — Nine   19 — Nineteen

10 — Ten   20 — Twenty

Number Words

Monday Monday Monday

Tuesday Tuesday Tuesday

Wednesday Wednesday Wednesday

Thursday Thursday Thursday

Friday Friday Friday

Saturday Saturday Saturday

Sunday Sunday Sunday

Days of the Week

Months of the year

January January January

February February February

March March March

April April April

May May May

June June June

July July July

August August August

September September September

October October October

November November November

December December December

Seconds   Seconds   Seconds

Minutes   Minutes   Minutes

Hours   Hours   Hours

Days   Days   Days

Weeks   Weeks   Weeks

Months   Months   Months

Years   Years   Years

Decades   Decades   Decades

Centuries   Centuries   Centuries

Millennia   Millennia   Millennia

Part 4:
Sentences

We will now practice writing
sentences using a smaller letter size.

Trace the dotted pangrams, affirmations, quotes
and then practice writing them on your own.

You can try writing your own affirmations &
quotes on the blank sheet(s)
at the end of this part!

Use your best handwriting!

Great Going!

My name is

My name is

I love to read and write.

I love to read and write.

I can write sentences in cursive font.

I can write sentences in cursive font.

My handwriting is neat and legible.

My handwriting is neat and legible.

Write your own sentences here:

How quickly daft jumping zebras vex.

Pangram: A pangram is a sentence that contains every letter of the alphabet at least once. Practice these fun lines.

Two driven jocks help fax my big quiz.

Sphinx of black quartz, judge my vow!

Fix problem quickly with galvanized jets.

The five boxing wizards jump quickly.

The quick brown fox jumps over a lazy dog.

Write your own Pangram here:

I love myself.

I am an amazing person.

I don't need to be perfect.

I am worthy of greatness.

I live each day to the fullest.

I celebrate my individuality.

Today is going to be a good day.

My potential to succeed is infinite.

Today, I will walk through my fears.

I can get through anything.

I can make a difference.

I am my own superhero.

I set goals and I reach them.

I have courage and confidence.

I am smart, capable and valuable.

I love and enjoy everything I do.

I have the power to create change.

I will become what I know I can be.

I trust myself.

I am proud of my own success.

I am focused, persistent and will never quit.

I take pride in the progress I make each day.

I am in charge of my own happiness.

I take pride in the progress I make each day.

I respect and treat myself with kindness and love.

I am beautiful on the outside as I am on the inside.

"The journey of a thousand miles begins with one step." — Lao Tzu

"You must be the change you wish to see in the world." — Mahatma Gandhi

"Make each day your masterpiece." — John Wooden

"Action is the foundational key to all success." — Pablo Picasso

"We are what we repeatedly do. Excellence, then,
is not an act, but a habit." — Aristotle

"Give every day the chance to become the most
beautiful day of your life." — Mark Twain

"Success occurs when opportunity meets
preparation." — Zig Ziglar

"Enjoy the little things, for one day you may
look back and realize they were the big things."
— Robert Brault

"The difference between ordinary and extraordinary is that little extra." — Jimmy Johnson

"Your imagination is your preview of life's coming attractions." — Albert Einstein

"Don't wait. The time will never be just right." — Napoleon Hill

"I will go anywhere as long as it is forward." — David Livingston

"If you can believe it, the mind can achieve it."
— Ronnie Lott

"Everything is practice." — Bill Shankley

"The harder I work, the luckier I get."
— Gary Player

"A champion is someone who gets up when
he can't." — Jack Dempsey

"Dream big and dare to fail." — Norman Vaughan

"Begin by always expecting good things to happen." — Tom Hopkins

"Don't watch the clock; do what it does. Keep going." — Sam Levenson

"Well done is better than well said." — Benjamin Franklin

"If opportunity doesn't knock, build a door." — Milton Berle

"Your time is limited, so don't waste it living someone else's life." — Steve Jobs

"An obstacle is often a stepping stone." —William Prescott

"Your attitude, not your aptitude, will determine your altitude." — Zig Ziglar

"The ladder of success is best climbed by stepping on the rungs of opportunity." - Ayn Rand

"Courage is never to let your actions be influenced by your fears." — Arthur Koestler

"Energy and persistence conquer all things." — Benjamin Franklin

"Tough times never last, but tough people do." — Dr. Robert Schuller

"Happiness is not something readymade. It comes from your own actions." — Dalai Lama

"Give every day the chance to become the most beautiful day of your life." — Mark Twain

"What we dwell on is who we become." — Oprah Winfrey

"Everything is practice." — Bill Shankley

"I am not a product of my circumstances. I am a product of my decisions." — Stephen Covey

"The only way to do great work is to love what you do." — Steve Jobs

"Though no one can go back and make a brand new start, anyone can start from now and make a brand new ending." — Carl Bard

"Success is the sum of small efforts repeated day in and day out." — Robert Collier

"Either you run the day, or the day runs you." — Jim Rohn

Part 5:
Poetry

Trace the definition of poetic forms and the poems by famous poets.
Practice writing them on your own on the blank page provided on the right handed side.

Use your best handwriting!

You are brilliant!

Definitions:

SONNET: Sonnet is a poem of fourteen lines using any of a number of formal rhyme schemes, having ten syllables per line.

HAIKU: Haiku is a Japanese poem of seventeen syllables, in three lines of five, seven, and five, traditionally evoking images of the natural world.

ODE: Ode is a lyric poem in the form of an address to a particular subject, often elevated in style or manner and written in varied or irregular meter.

ACROSTIC: Acrostic is a poem, word puzzle, or other composition in which certain letters in each line form word(s).

EPIC: Epic is a long poem narrating the deeds and adventures of heroic or legendary figures or the history of a nation.

Definitions:

FREE VERSE: Free verse is poetry that does not rhyme or have a regular meter.

RHYME: A rhyme is a poem composed of lines that end in words or syllables with sounds that correspond with those at the ends of other lines.

BALLAD: A ballad is a poem narrating a story in short stanzas. Traditional ballads are typically of unknown authorship, having been passed on orally from one generation to the next as part of the folk culture.

LIMERICK: A limerick is a humorous verse frequently bawdy, of three long and two short lines rhyming AABBA.

NARRATIVE: A narrative poem in literature is a poem which tells a story through verse. It has plot, characters, and setting.

The Road Not Taken
— Robert Frost

Two roads diverged in a yellow wood,

And sorry I could not travel both

And be one traveler, long I stood

And looked down one as far as I could

To where it bent in the undergrowth;

Then took the other, as just as fair,

And having perhaps the better claim,

Though as for that the passing there

Had worn them really about the same,

And both that morning equally lay

Oh, I kept the first for another day!

Yet knowing how way leads on to way,

I doubted if I should ever come back.

The Road Not Taken (Continued ...)
— Robert Frost

I shall be telling this with a sigh

Somewhere ages and ages hence:

Two roads diverged in a wood, and I

I took the one less traveled by,

And that has made all the difference.

— * —

The Echoing Green

— William Blake

The Sun does arise,

And make happy the skies.

The merry bells ring

To welcome the Spring.

The sky-lark and thrush,

The birds of the bush,

Sing louder around,

To the bells' cheerful sound.

While our sports shall be seen

On the Echoing Green.

Old John with white hair

Does laugh away care,

Sitting under the oak,

Among the old folk,

They laugh at our play,

The Echoing Green (Continued)

And soon they all say,

Such such were the joys.

When we all --girls and boys--

In our youth-time were seen,

The sky-lark and thrush,

On the Echoing Green.

Till the little ones weary

No more can be merry

The sun does descend,

And our sports have an end:

Round the laps of their mothers,

Many sisters and brothers,

Like birds in their nest,

Are ready for rest;

And sport no more seen,

On the darkening Green.

William Blake was an English poet, painter and printmaker. Blake is held in high regard by later critics for his expressiveness and creativity, and for the philosophical and mystical undercurrents within his work. He is now considered a seminal figure in the history of the poetry and visual arts of the Romantic Age.

___ * ___

Robert Lee Frost was an American poet. His work was initially published in England before it was published in the United States. Frost was honored frequently during his lifetime and is the only poet to receive four Pulitzer Prizes for Poetry. He was awarded the Congressional Gold Medal in 1960 for his poetic works. On July 22, 1961, Frost was named poet laureate of Vermont.

Part 6:
Famous People

Trace the famous words by
William Shakespeare, Madame Curie
and Thomas Edison.

Famous Speeches

Trace the famous speeches.
Practice writing them on your own
on the blank page provided on
the right handed side.

Fantastic!

William Shakespeare

Famous quotes:

"All that glitters is not gold."

-The Merchant of Venice, Act II, Scene VII

"Action is eloquence."

——Volumnia in Coriolanus, Act III, Scene II

"What's in a name? That which we call a rose

By any other word would smell as sweet..."

-Romeo and Juliet, Act II, Scene II

"All the worlds a stage,

And all the men and women merely players:

They have their exits and their entrances;

And one man in his time plays many parts."

-As You Like It, Act II, Scene VII

William Shakespeare

Famous quotes:

"Some are born great, some achieve greatness,

and some have greatness thrust upon them."

—Malvolio in Twelfth Night, Act II, Scene V

"Our doubts are traitors,

And make us lose the good we oft might win,

By fearing to attempt."

—Lucio in Measure for Measure, Act I, Scene IV

"There is nothing either good or bad,

but thinking makes it so."

—Hamlet in Hamlet, Act II, Scene II

"The miserable have no other medicine,

but only hope." —Claudio in Measure for

Measure, Act III, Scene I

Practice writing these quotes

© Sujatha Lalgudi   ISBN: 979-8654857675

Madame Marie Curie (1867 – 1934)

She was a Polish and naturalized-French physicist and chemist who conducted pioneering research on radioactivity. She was the first woman to become a professor at the University of Paris in 1906, the first woman to win a Nobel prize, and the only person to win the Nobel Prize in two scientific fields. She shared the 1903 Nobel Prize in Physics with Pierre Curie and with the physicist Henri Becquerel for their pioneering work developing the theory of "radioactivity" — a term she coined.

Marie won the 1911 Nobel Prize in Chemistry for her discovery of the elements polonium and radium. In addition to her Nobel Prizes, she has received numerous other honours and tributes.

Quotes by Madame Curie:

"Be less curious about people and more curious about ideas."

"Nothing in life is to be feared, it is only to be understood. Now is the time to understand more, so that we may fear less."

"It is my earnest desire that some of you should carry on this scientific work and keep for your ambition the determination to make a permanent contribution to science."

"I am among those who think that science has great beauty. A scientist in his laboratory is not only a technician: he is also a child placed before natural phenomena which impress him like a fairy tale."

"We must not forget that when radium was discovered no one knew that it would prove useful in hospitals. The work was one of pure science. And this is a proof that scientific work must not be considered from the point of view of the direct usefulness of it. It must be done for itself, for the beauty of science, and then there is always the chance that a scientific discovery may become like the radium a benefit for humanity."

Quotes by Thomas Edison

"A genius is often merely a talented person who has done all of his or her homework."

"When I have finally decided that a result is worth getting, I go ahead on it and make trial after trial until it comes."

"I find out what the world needs. Then I go ahead and try to invent it."

"Opportunity is missed by most people because it is dressed in overalls and looks like work."

"If we all did the things we are really capable of doing, we would literally astound ourselves..."

"To invent, you need a good imagination and a pile of junk."

"I never did a day's work in my life, it was all fun."

"I have not failed. I've just found 10,000 ways that won't work."

Thomas Alva Edison (1847–1931)

He was an American inventor and businessman.

He developed many devices in fields such as electric power generation, mass communication, sound recording, and motion pictures.

He created the world's first industrial research laboratory. One of the most famous and prolific inventors of all time, Thomas Alva Edison exerted a tremendous influence on modern life, contributing inventions such as the incandescent light bulb, the phonograph, and the motion picture camera, as well as improving the telegraph and telephone. In his 84 years, he acquired an astounding 1,093 patents.

Aside from being an inventor, Edison also managed to become a successful manufacturer and businessman, marketing his inventions to the public.

Moon Speech
September 12, 1962, Rice University
— John F. Kennedy

"We choose to go to the moon. We choose to go to the moon in this decade and do the other things, not because they are easy, but because they are hard; because that goal will serve to organize and measure the best of our energies and skills, because that challenge is one that we are willing to accept, one we are unwilling to postpone, and one we intend to win, and the others, too.

We have had our failures, but so have others, even if they do not admit them. And they may be less public.

Well, space is there, and we're going to climb it, and the moon and the planets are there, and new hopes for knowledge and peace are there.

I Have a Dream

August 28, 1963 – Lincoln Memorial

– Martin Luther King, Jr.

"I say to you today, my friends, so even though we face the difficulties of today and tomorrow, I still have a dream.

It is a dream deeply rooted in the American dream.

I have a dream that one day this nation will rise up and live out the true meaning of its creed: 'We hold these truths to be self-evident, that all men are created equal.' I have a dream today. This is our hope. . . With this faith we will be able to hew out of the mountain of despair a stone of hope. With this faith we will be able to transform the jangling discords of our nation into a beautiful symphony of brotherhood.

Commencement Address

June 4, 1982 – Wellesley College, Mass

– Maya Angelou

Graduates,

Now the joy begins. Now the work begins.

The years of preparation, of tedious study and

exciting learning at least begin to make sense.

The jumble of words and the tangle of small

and great thoughts begin to take order, and this

morning you can see a small portion, an

infinitesimal portion, of the map of your future...

...you have still had to develop an outstanding

courage to invent this moment, for you have

invented it. Of all your attributes –

your youth, your beauty, your wit,

your kindnesses, your money –

courage is indeed your greatest achievement.

It is the greatest of all your virtues, for without

Commencement Address (Continued...)
courage you cannot practice any other virtue
with consistency.
And now that you have shown that you are
capable of manufacturing that important and
wondrous virtue, you must be asking yourselves
what you will do with it. Be assured that
that question is in the minds of your parents, of
your instructors, of people whose names you
will never know, of the group of women who
will sit in those very seats next year.
Since you have worked this hard, since you have
also been greatly blessed, since you are here, you
have developed a marvelous level of courage, and
the question then which you must ask yourself,
I think, is will you really do the job which is to
be done: Make this country more than it is
today

Commencement Address (Continued...)

...It takes a phenomenal amount of courage. You may lean against it, it will hold you up, you have that. And the joy of achievement, the ecstasy of achievement. It enlightens and lightens at the same time. It is a marvelous thing. Today, your joy begins, today your work begins. You are phenomenal.

It is upon you to increase your virtue, the virtue of courage—it is upon you. You will be challenged mightily, and you will fall many times. But it is important to remember that it may be necessary to encounter defeat, I don't know. But I do know that a diamond, one of the most precious elements in this planet, certainly one in many ways the hardest, is the result of extreme pressure, and time. Under less pressure, it's crystal. Less pressure than that, its

coal, less than that, its fossilized leaves are just plain dirt.

You must encounter, confront life. There is no person here who is over one year old who hasn't slept with fear, or pain or loss or grief, or terror, and yet we have all arisen, have made whatever absolutions we were able to, or chose to, dressed, and said to other human beings, "Good morning. How are you? Fine, thanks." Therein lies our chance toward nobleness —not nobility —but nobleness, the best of a human being is in that ability to overcome.

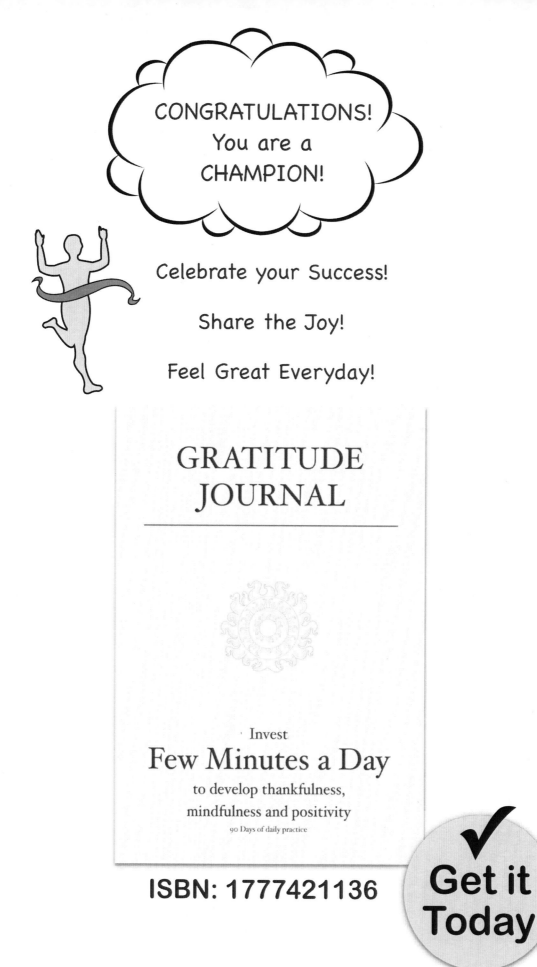

CONGRATULATIONS!
You are a
CHAMPION!

Celebrate your Success!

Share the Joy!

Feel Great Everyday!

GRATITUDE
JOURNAL

Invest
Few Minutes a Day
to develop thankfulness,
mindfulness and positivity
90 Days of daily practice

ISBN: 1777421136

Get it Today

Write to me at **sujatha.lalgudi@gmail.com** with the subject:

Teen Cursive along with **your name** to receive:

- Additional practice worksheets.
- A name tracing worksheet so you can practice writing your own name.
- An Award Certificate in Color to reward yourself!

- -

CERTIFICATE

WRITING SUPERSTAR

THIS CERTIFICATE IS PRESENTED TO

_____

HANDWRITING PENMANSHIP

HIPPIDOO
PENMANSHIP

_____   _____
DATE   SIGNATURE

Made in United States
North Haven, CT
01 February 2023

31959350R00061